How to Evaluate Your Middle School

A Practitioner's Guide
for an Informal Program Evaluation

By Sandra L. Schurr

NATIONAL MIDDLE SCHOOL ASSOCIATION

National Middle School Association
2600 Corporate Exchange Drive, Suite 370
Columbus, Ohio 43231-1672

Sandra L. Schurr has made many contributions to middle school education. Among these are her practical publications for National Middle School Association. An Associate Professor at the University of South Florida, Schurr is Middle Grades Director, National Resource Center for Middle Grades Education, located at USF. NMSA is pleased to be able to publish the work of this dynamic former middle school teacher and administrator.

Recognition is also due Lucy Smith of the National Resource Center and Mary Mitchell for assistance in designing, proofing, and preparing the manuscript for printing.

ISBN: 1-56090-072-5

This book is dedicated to the special mentors in my professional life who have helped me "evaluate" my work and grow in the process — Jim Fox, Dick Puglisi, Howard Johnston, and John Lounsbury.

Contents

Foreword

Assessment of school programs is an essential component of the effective middle level school. Educators, community leaders, and citizens cry out for a means of measuring the effectiveness of their schools. The preponderance of the literature suggests that a review of test scores and other quantitative data is the route to program evaluation. Sadly, there is a void with little regard being given for other more broadly informative strategies for assessing the effectiveness of school programs.

This monograph fills this void. In it Sandra Schurr provides insights into a tough topic while assuring that the suggestions and strategies are useful to both practitioner and researcher. The emphasis in this work is on generating both qualitative and quantitative data which are clear, insightful, and relevant to teachers, principals, parents, and citizens.

The format of this monograph serves as a step-by-step guide to conducting a meaningful assessment of a middle level program. Each section reviews current thinking regarding a topic and offers a series of questions for the school evaluation team to answer as next steps are considered. This opportunity for the reader both to learn and reflect on the evaluation process sets this volume apart from other literature on school assessment.

Too often educators shy away from asking and answering the tough questions about their school's program. A focussed school improvement project that seeks improved student achievement requires that these questions be addressed. *How To Evaluate Your Middle School* provides a much-needed guide for middle level educators to work aggressively and collaboratively at providing answers to the tough questions. It provides strategies for using derived answers to maintain a focus on the development and implementation of educational experiences appropriate to early adolescents. Therein lies its greatest value.

— **Ronald Williamson**
Executive Director
National Middle School Association

Introduction

Why Was This Book Written?

One can't develop, implement, nurture, refine, or improve a middle school program without an evaluation component in mind. The essential elements of a middle school program should drive the evaluation process rather than the evaluation procedures driving the way a middle school does business. Although this position should be obvious, the reality is that many schools assess their status only on such things as student achievement scores, numbers of retentions or suspensions, or percentages of students making the honor rolls.

Although numerical and objective figures are an important part of the evaluation process, they should not become ends in themselves. A fair evaluation must be supported by other methods of assessment including attitude surveys, personal interviews, formal observations, individual checklists, and shadow studies of students. These evaluation tools and techniques provide valuable means of clarifying statistical data and also support efforts to bring about needed changes.

This publication provides middle level educators at the school site with a variety of options for conducting their own self-evaluation, for assessing how well they are doing in the pursuit of excellence at the middle level. It is also intended to make evaluation a manageable process in terms of available time, energy, cost, and expertise. In this age of school accountability with state and national assessments, teacher empowerment, and site-based management the emphasis on evaluation needs to come from within — from the bottom up — and from the heart as well as the mind.

Who Should Use This Book?

This monograph is written explicitly for practitioners, for teachers and principals in an individual school. It is written in a language that should have special appeal for the the non-expert who wants to experiment with the elements of evaluation in order to discover the real benefits that can come from a meaningful evaluation effort. The book has been created to provide a set of guidelines for conducting an informal, in-house evaluation by a school-based improvement team. Although outside consultants may be used as part of the process, there is much more to be gained from an in-house process which increases acceptance of results. All stakeholders in the school community should be represented in some way as part of the evaluation team or effort so that students, teachers, administrators, support staff, parents, and taxpayers can all have a part in making their school a better place to work and learn.

What Can Be Gained From the Materials Included?

When a school decides to conduct its own self-study, it is important that the evaluation planners have access to basic information about the major elements of a meaningful evaluation program. Although not trained evaluators, the school's evaluation leadership team needs to become familiar with the essential elements of an effective evaluation. Members need to understand and be able to use basic evaluation terminology. They need to examine the various methods of data collection in order to develop a customized evaluation plan that fits the local situation. In addition they need to know how to interpret and make good use of the evaluation results. In short, even amateur school evaluators need to develop a working knowledge of both "the art and the science" of what goes into a school evaluation project.

How Is It Designed to be Used?

All members of a school faculty should become reasonably familiar with the contents of this monograph. They need to understand what is involved with a school-based evaluation effort. The most meaningful evaluation activities are those conducted by a team of "informed amateurs" who know enough about evaluation to be competent, but who are not discouraged by their limitations. Once a staff has internalized this material, decisions can take place to get the evaluation underway.

If we are to change education to meet the demands of the information age, we must overcome our habit of using product-oriented assessment techniques to measure process-oriented education. We need to redesign assessment to fit the goal of the restructured school ... (Therefore), we must expand the range and variety of the assessment techniques we use.

— A.L. Costa

1

Why EvaluateYour Middle Level Program?

Here's What We Think

Unfortunately, when educators hear the terms *evaluation, assessment, measurement,* or *accountability* many negative connotations surface in their minds. We tend to equate such concepts with test anxiety, with predetermined failure, with internal stress, and with personal frustration rather than with an air of optimism and enthusiasm for self or program diagnosis and ultimately school-improvement. The reasons for this condition are many.

To begin with, many educational decisions are based on incomplete evaluation results or inconclusive evidence. Confusion as to both the role of and the dichotomy of formative and summative evaluation procedures and the inability of scholars to reach consensus as to their precise meaning have often confused those responsible for its implementation. Too, one often forgets that evaluation is not an end in itself, but should serve as an important springboard for looking at the discrepancy between "what is" and "what should be." Evaluation is intended to be ongoing, never-ending, and self-perpetuating. It is never static.

In addition, pressure from the tax-paying community, from local or state legislators, and from central office personnel forces hasty decisions that are counterproductive to the long-term goals of the organization. It is time that we put long range plans and expectations before instant (but false) gratification or unrealistic deadlines to solve long-standing problems. Finally, misuse or overuse of test results can take a disproportionate amount of time and energy from the primary business of teaching. Only through the widespread participation and commitment of all those affected by the evaluation outcomes, will the desired individual growth and change occur.

To use this handbook effectively, it is important that we have a common nomenclature. To distinguish among the varied terms, we will take the position of Choppin (1990) who states that "measurement" requires the assigning of a numerical quantity to some element and is rarely carried out for its own sake. Although it may be included in an assessment or evaluation, it is more to be regarded as a basic research procedure. Similarly, he takes the stance that "assessment" should be reserved for application to people and not to programs. Therefore, that leaves the term "evaluation" as the purpose for this publication because it applies to abstract entities such as programs, curricula, and organizational variables. This, of course, implies making a comparison to other programs, curricula, and organizational patterns.

Reasons for Evaluating

To get an evaluation project off the ground it is desirable to identify the many reasons or purposes for doing an evaluation. Worthen (1990) suggests that most program evaluators agree that a constructive program evaluation can play either a formative purpose (helping to improve the program) or a summative purpose (deciding whether a program should be continued). He also cites six possible reasons for spending time on program evaluations:

(1) decisions about program installation;
(2) decisions about program continuation or expansion;
(3) decisions about program modification;
(4) gathering evidence to rally support for a program;
(5) gathering evidence to rally opposition to a program; and
(6) contributing to the understanding of basic psychological, social and similar processes associated with the program.

Formal evaluation of any middle school can be a very time-consuming, expensive, and complicated process. Although there is much to be gained from such an expenditure of resources, we believe that most schools would rather conduct an informal, in-house, and inexpensive evaluation that is compatible with today's emphasis on school-based management.

Evaluation, of course, always involves some risk on the part of the evaluators because of both limitations or impediments of current program evaluation models and procedures. In some cases, for example, evaluation efforts lack an adequate knowledge base. In other cases, program evaluators fail to understand the political and affective nature of evaluation approaches and techniques either because of ignorance, inadequate training, or limited resources.

In spite of these variables, much is to be gained by conducting an evaluation that involves all stakeholders as long as it can be manageable, informative, and can lead to needed changes. Approaching the evaluation of one's workplace, one's home away from

home, or one's community center should be a positive and rewarding experience for all involved. Anything less than this perception on the part of staff, administration, students, or parents will only inhibit the activities and taint the findings. The challenge, then, becomes one of widespread participation of all individuals associated with the formal education process.

REFERENCES

Brinkerhoff, R. O., Brethower, D. M., Hluchyj, T., & Nowakowski, J. R. (1983). *Program evaluation: A practitioner's guide for trainers and educators.* Boston: Kluwer-Nijhoff.

Choppin, B. H. (1990). Evaluation as a field of inquiry. In Walberg, H. J. & Haertel, G. D. (Eds.). (1990). *The international encyclopedia of educational evaluation.* New York: Pergamon Press.

Eichhorn, D. H. (1987). *The middle school.* Columbus, OH: National Middle School Association

Lounsbury, J. H., & Johnston, J. H. (1988). *Life in the three sixth grades.* Reston, VA: National Association of Secondary School Principals

National Association of Secondary School Principals, Council on Middle Level Education. (1985). *Assessing excellence: A guide for studying the middle level school.* Reston, VA: National Association of Secondary School Principals.

Worthen, B. R. (1990). Program evaluation. In Walberg, H. J. & Haertel, G. D. (Eds.). (1990). *The international encyclopedia of educational evaluation.* New York: Pergamon Press.

Worthen, B. R. & Sanders, J. R. (1987). *Education evaluation: Alternative approaches and practical guidelines.* New York: Longman.

What Do You Think?

Questions to Consider

1. What elements of our middle level program do we want to evaluate?

2. What reasons/purposes do we have for wanting to evaluate each of these program components?

3. What will we do with these evaluation elements and how will we involve them in the evaluation process?

4. Who are the stakeholders for each of these evaluation elements; how will we involve them in the evaluation process?

5. What resources (people, dollars, data sources, etc.) are available to us in conducting this evaluation process?

6. What tools and techniques are available to us in conducting this evaluation process?

7. What indicators will we use in conducting the evaluation for each of the program components? What criteria will be established to determine "what is" and "what should be?"

8. How will we coordinate the evaluation process and obtain meaningful consensus on evaluation standards, findings, and recommendations?

9. How will we establish a positive and constructive climate for evaluation to take place in our school?

10. What is the most effective way to disseminate the evaluation results and obtain input from those involved?

2

What Are the Program Components of an Exemplary Middle School?

Here's What We Think

The seeds of the middle school concept were first planted and took root during the early 1960s. This was an exciting time for educational innovation. Change was spawned by everything from the launch of Sputnik to the implementation of new math. According to Eichhorn (1987), the middle school movement began for four reasons:

(1) A recognition and reaffirmation of the belief that youngsters aged 10-14 are in a unique stage of development in which they share similar physical, mental, social, and emotional characteristics;

(2) New medical evidence that suggests that youngsters attain puberty at an earlier age than before;

(3) Forces such as the new technology, racial integration, and the knowledge explosion that were affecting society; and

(4) The junior high school organization was perceived as, and in many instances had become, an institution patterned after the senior high school.

Although the middle school concept became a viable organizational pattern for restructuring many junior highs during the 60s and early 70s, it did not begin to reach its full potential until a few years later when societal conditions provided an additional impetus for significant

change. Together these forces provided the critical mass needed to ensure lasting change. That is to say, the chain reaction of restructuring middle level schools did not become an accelerated landslide until the 1980s when leaders in health, social sciences, education, and business professed mutual needs. Until then the idea was simply ahead of its time, but now their goals were in synch. The reasons for this are many.

To begin with, the family structure of the 60s was very different from the family structure of today. Families of the 60s tended to be more stable, traditional, structured, homogeneous, middle class, fiscally independent, secure and supportive of one another. They were also less mobile, less fragmented, less dependent on government, less fearful of the future, and less likely to be single or second parent homes. As a result, the middle school philosophy with its heavy emphasis on the needs and characteristics of the students, its interdisciplinary team or surrogate family concept, its attention to the affective domain through advisory time, and its passion for exploratory offerings were incompatible with the general mindset and perceptions of society in the 60s and what was viewed as the mission of schooling.

By contrast, the needs of today's family are very different and therefore require many new ways of educating the children. For example, job mobility, two-income families, single parents, and small non-extended families make the "house and/or team concept" a desirable dimension of schools. Likewise, the Information Age with its accelerated rate of change makes it virtually impossible for individuals or small, independent groups to survive but rather requires an attitude of interdependence and cooperation among diverse groups as well as time to teach some prosocial values and behaviors.

Another reason middle schools are more likely to succeed today than in the past has to do with changes in the workplace. During the industrial age, corporate America was hierarchical, fiercely competitive, autocratic, centralized, and obsessed with increased mass production of assembly line items. Today, these attributes are no longer valued but have been largely replaced with such notions as decentralization of decision-making, empowerment of workers, teaming in the workplace, and concern for employee health, safety, and life styles. The middle school now can become a more desirable partner with the business community since it shares many of the same goals and methods of operation.

The *Turning Points* Recommendations

A third reason middle schools will become a "way of life" in the education of American youth in the 21st century is because there now exist both a national mandate and a national forum for its message and programs. The Carnegie Corporation's Report *Turning Points* received nation-wide recognition and acceptance when initially released in June, 1989. The recommendations contained in this report call for middle grade schools that:

1. **Create small communities for learning** where stable, close, mutually respectful relationships with adults and peers are considered fundamental for intellectual development and personal growth. The key elements of these communities are schools-within-schools or houses, stu-

dents, and teachers grouped together as teams, and small group advisories that ensure that every student is known well by at least one adult.

2. **Teach a core academic program** that results in students who are literate, including in the sciences, and who know how to think critically, lead a healthy life, behave ethically, and assume the responsibilities of citizenship in a pluralistic society. Youth service to promote values for citizenship is an essential part of the core academic program.

3. **Ensure success for all students** through elimination of tracking by achievement level and promotion of cooperative learning, flexibility in arranging instructional time, and adequate resources (time, space, equipment, and materials) for teachers.

4. **Empower teachers and administrators to make decisions about the experiences of middle grade students** through creative control by teachers over the instructional program linked to greater responsibilities for students' performance, governance committees that assist the principal in designing and coordinating school-wide programs, and autonomy and leadership within sub-schools or houses to create environments tailored to enhance the intellectual and emotional development of all youth.

5. **Staff middle grade schools with teachers who are expert at teaching young adolescents** and who have been specially prepared for assignment to the middle grades.

6. **Improve academic performance through fostering the health and fitness** of young adolescents, by providing a health coordinator in every middle grade school, access to health care and

counseling services, and a health-promoting school environment.

7. **Reengage families in the education of young adolescents** by giving families meaningful roles in school governance, communicating with families about the school program and student's progress, and offering families opportunities to support the learning process at home and at the school.

8. **Connect schools with communities,** which together share responsibility for each middle grade student's success, through identifying service opportunities in the community, establishing partnerships and collaborations to ensure students' access to health and social services, and using community resources to enrich the instructional program and opportunities for constructive after-school activities.

Widespread Support Now Exists

In the 1960s we did not have several national associations or organizations dedicated to the education of early adolescents as we have in the 1990s. The National Middle School Association, the National Association of Secondary School Principals, the Center for Early Adolescence, and the National Resource Center for Middle Grades Education are all strong and active proponents for restructuring the outdated junior high school program into a middle school organizational pattern. There are also strong state middle school associations advancing the cause. These various national and state groups are collaborating with one another to support and implement school reform through development of quality research, publications, training programs, and networks. This universal effort throughout the United States and Europe will transform the education of early adolescents well into the next century.

Characteristics of Exemplary Middle Schools

A consensus has emerged among today's middle level educators about what a good middle level school is like. The following characteristics are most commonly identified:

1. a philosophy based on the unique needs and characteristics of the early adolescent

2. educators knowledgeable about and committed to teaching the early adolescent

3. a curriculum balanced between the cognitive (subject-centered) and affective (student-centered) needs of the early adolescent

4. teachers who use varied instructional strategies

5. a comprehensive teacher advisory program

6. an interdisciplinary team organization at all grades

7. a flexible block master schedule

8. a full exploratory program

9. both team planning and personal planning time for all teachers during the school day

10. a positive and collaborative school climate

11. shared decision-making where the people closest to the "client" are involved in the decision-making process of the school

12. a smooth transition process from elementary to middle school and from middle school to high school

13. intramurals, interest based mini-courses, clubs, and social events

14. a physical plant that accommodates teams and provides spaces for both small and large group meetings

15. a commitment to the importance of health and physical fitness for all students on a regular and full basis

16. a commitment to involving families in the education of early adolescents by not only keeping them informed of student progress and school programs but by giving them meaningful roles in the schooling process

17. a positive connection between school and the community through student service projects, business partnerships, and full use of community resources within the school curriculum

18. consistent use of cooperative learning strategies in the classroom

19. an emphasis on the use of higher order thinking skills and hands-on instructional strategies

20. the involvement and empowerment of students wherever possible to do so

These middle school characteristics could become specific elements to be evaluated.

REFERENCES

Eichhorn, D. H. (1987). *The middle school.* Columbus, OH: National Middle School Association.

Turning Points: Preparing American youth for the 21st Century. (1989). New York: The Carnegie Corporation of New York.

What Do You Think?

Questions to Consider

1. How would you describe a typical student in physical characteristics, behaviors, attitudes, and interests?

2. How would such a profile of a student in your school have looked like 10-20 years ago?

3. Which of the 20 characteristics listed for an exemplary middle school would be most important to have in your setting and why?

4. Which of the 20 characteristics listed would be least important to have in your setting and why?

5. Using a four point scale rate your school's implementation of each of the 20 characteristics.

   1-Full Implementation
   2-Partial Implementation
   3-Little Implementation
   4-No Implementation

6. For each of the 20 characteristics rated a 1 or 2 how would you describe the quality of implementation for that characteristic?

7. Which of the 20 characteristics would be most difficult to develop in your school setting? Give reasons for your response.

8. Which of the identified 20 characteristics would be most easily developed in your school setting? Give reasons for your response.

9. How might priorities be set for building a school that ultimately would incorporate all 20 characteristics?

10. How will you know when you have reached your goal?

3

When Do You Involve Others in the Evaluation?

Here's What We Think

The evaluation process provides educators with information they need to help improve educational programs and practices. As indicated in the first section, recognition of this fact has often placed undue pressures on school personnel to evaluate anything and everything, often for political rather than educational reasons. It is our premise that the more practitioners become involved with the evaluation process, the more supportive they will become in acknowledging its essential role, participating in its varied tasks, and utilizing its findings.

Although evaluation is sometimes highly systematic, structured, and objective, it can also take on a more informal approach. Informal evaluation is often the only practical approach. Informal evaluation involves choices that are highly subjective. Such subjectivity, however, is important if only because it allows for maximum flexibility in customizing an evaluation plan to suit the characteristics and demographics of a given school site and because it allows for maximum ownership of all stakeholder groups in that evaluation process.

There are five major factors to be considered when developing an evaluation plan for a program — goals, stakeholders, audiences, control, and timing. The first dimension addresses the question "what," the second and third dimensions address the question "who," the fourth dimension addresses the question "how," and the last dimension addresses the question "when." Each one of these is discussed in turn.

Goal-Setting

Any evaluation program should be launched by establishing goals and clarifying what is expected to happen. NASSP's Council on Middle Level Education (1988) suggests that there are four categories or types of goals that one can consider. *Diagnostic evaluations* (p. 4) are designed to help us understand the discrepancies that exist between some ideal state and where we actually are. In other words, diagnostic evaluations help us to see where an intervention might be needed in order to bring about a more desirable set of circumstances for our clients.

Monitoring and accountability evaluations (p. 6) stem from our need to determine whether a program is performing as promised and ask the question: "Is the program serving the people it was designed to serve?" Monitoring evaluations, on the other hand, assume that a need was identified and that a program was implemented with the necessary elements it was supposed to contain. It asks the question: "Is the program being conducted as promised?"

Impact evaluations (p. 7) help us determine if a program is achieving its intended outcomes. Since most programs are goal-directed, impact evaluations are designed to determine if our goals are being met, to what extent they are being met, and if the outcomes can, in fact, be attributed to the program.

Finally, *cost-benefit evaluations* (p. 10) help determine if we are getting our money's worth out of a program. They tell us how much it costs to achieve some unit of benefit.

In summary, when planning an evaluation project the team must establish the ultimate goal for conducting the evaluation in terms of desired outcomes which focus on diagnostic, accountability, impact, or cost benefit factors.

Identifying Stakeholders

Stakeholders refer to those individuals who have the most to win or lose from the evaluations' findings. They are the ones directly affected by the results. Stakeholders can be clients, sponsors, or participants of the program itself. Generally speaking, an evaluation project's sponsor is the agency or person who authorizes and funds the project while the client is the specific group for whom the evaluation is intended. In essence, a stakeholder is anyone who has a material interest in the program outcome and would benefit or lose if the program were eliminated. It is important for the evaluation team to obtain a variety of viewpoints when collecting information from all its target populations. Therefore, the questions, concerns, and values of the stakeholders must be integral parts of the evaluation process.

Identifying Audiences

Audiences refer to those groups who will receive the results and, presumably, have an interest in them. It is imperative that the evaluation team understand the diverse audiences the school serves so that the evaluation legitimately addresses the kinds of concerns all groups are likely to have. In disseminating evaluation results to the varied audiences, Brinkerhoff and his colleagues (1983) state that an evaluation program to be defensible must meet these criteria:

1. It is clear. (It is understood by important audiences.)

2. It is accessible. (It is disseminated to those who have a right to know.)

3. It is useful. (It is intended to meet an information need that will serve the program.)

4. It is relevant. (It is timely and realistic in serving the requirements of students.)

5. It is humane. (It can be accomplished without harming those involved or affected.)

6. It is compatible. (It is congruent with the goals of the sponsor, client, participants, and stakeholders.)

7. It is worthwhile. (Its probable benefit justifies its probable costs.)

Control of Data

Once a decision has been made as to the purposes or goals of an evaluation project and who are its intended stakeholders and audiences, it is time to consider who should conduct the evaluation itself and who should control the data sources and measures. Again, Brinkerhoff and colleagues (1983) suggest that the control issue be flexible and participatory in nature. External or outside evaluators are discouraged if one is to conduct an in-house, self-evaluation study in which the process is as important as the end product and the measures will be informal, frequent, diverse, and internal. Sample sizes will most likely be relatively small. The questions to be answered are simply: (1) What is working? (2) What needs to be improved? and (3) How can it be improved?

Alloting Time

A final element to consider has to do with time. Time has to be allocated for the actual implementation of the evaluation plan. The ideal time for the evaluation activities to take place also has to be determined. Again, there is no right or wrong way to make these decisions. Two things that always need to be considered in deciding are what information is needed and when that information must be made available.

REFERENCES

Brinkerhoff, R. O., Brethower, D. M., Hluchyj, T., & Nowakowski, J. R. (1983). *Program evaluation: A practitioner's guide for trainers and educators.* Boston: Kluwer-Nijhoff.

National Association of Secondary School Principlals , Council on Middle Level Education. (1988). *Assessing excellence: A guide for studying the middle level school.* Reston, VA: National Association of Secondary School Principals.

Creativity requires the freedom to consider "unthinkable" alternatives, to doubt the worth of cherished practices.

———

I am entirely certain that twenty years from now we will look back at education as it is practiced in most schools today and wonder that we could have tolerated anything so primitive.

— John W. Gardner

What Do You Think?

Questions to Consider

1. What is the primary goal or purpose for evaluating each of our program components?

2. Is our goal or purpose clear? What evidence do we have?

3. Is our goal or purpose accessible? What evidence do we have?

4. Is our goal or purpose useful? What evidence do we have?

5. Is our goal or purpose relevant? What evidence do we have?

6. Is our goal or purpose humane? What evidence do we have?

7. Is our goal or purpose compatible? What evidence do we have?

8. Is our goal or purpose worthwhile? What evidence do we have?

9. Who are the stakeholders in each of our program components?

10. Who are the clients in each of our program components? Are they also stakeholders?

11. Who are the intended audiences for each of our program components? Are they also clients and stakeholders?

12. What guidelines for control of resources and data measures will we establish for each of our program components?

13. What time constraints and timelines are to be considered for each of our program components?

14. What is our next step?

4

What Alternative Evaluation Tools and Techniques Are Available?

Here's What We Think

This section provides the reader with a menu of informal evaluation tools and techniques that can be parts of any school-based evaluation program. They vary in purpose and complexity which, in turn, affects the time required, the experience levels of the evaluators, and the budget constraints of the sponsors. The key dimension to consider first is the evaluation's goal or purpose which, in turn, will influence what evaluation practices will eventually be selected from options available.

No two school-based evaluations will or should look alike. Customizing the evaluation plan is critical to its success because each school site varies considerably in its characteristics and/or demographics. Factors to consider in creating a local plan include the following characteristics of a school:

1. Size (student and staff numbers)

2. Grade organization pattern

3. Instructional organization plan (teams? departments?)

4. Location

5. Current philosophical orientation (junior high? child-centered?)

6. Program (courses/activity options)

7. Population (ethnic, socioeconomic, and achievement backgrounds of students)

8. Expectations (levels of intended academic and affective achievements)

9. Norms (values, rituals of stakeholders)

10. School/community/parent relations (involvement and support from parents and taxpayers)

Another point for evaluation planners to keep in mind is that the evaluation tasks should never be viewed as ends in themselves, but merely as important checkpoints along a continuum of peaks and valleys. One thing every school can count on is change, and therefore the evaluation process needs to be ongoing in some way, shape, or form. Choosing a program component(s) to focus on each year is highly desirable and should be incorporated into the school's annual statement of goals and objectives.

Communication again becomes a key issue in making the evaluation both practical and pragmatic. The more a sense of ownership is created for the stakeholders, the more committed they will be in making the evaluation process work. Viewing evaluation as a positive force will go far in bringing about constructive leadership and valid results that will have real value in an age of accountability.

Surveys and Questionnaires

Perhaps the most common means of gathering data in any evaluation is that of the survey or questionnaire. Surveys and questionnaires have several advantages as data sources. These include the following:

1. Stakeholders are familiar with this strategy as they have most likely administered one and/or been a participant in several. They consider them "safe" and "non-threatening."

2. They are relatively inexpensive to administer. One can reach large numbers of people in a relatively short period of time. They do not require the use of outside observers or trained evaluators.

3. They can be administered at a convenient time for the participants and in almost any kind of space or location.

4. They can be designed to maintain the respondent's anonymity, a factor valued highly by most participants. Individuals are more likely to be honest in responding if they have assurance that there will be no repercussions regardless of their responses.

5. They can be standardized and uniform, both in the way they are constructed and the way they are administered. Again, this quality is desirable in many situations because it does assure some degree of continuity and quality control both in the way the data are collected and the way the information is compiled.

Guidelines for Constructing Survey Instruments

Although there is much literature available on the construction of survey questionnaires, a few important suggestions are outlined below for the reader's reference.

1. Is the questionnaire layout inviting and readable?

2. Are the directions/instructions/procedures clear?

3. Are there adequate questions to cover major issues?

4. Is there a logical sequencing of questions and are those questions grouped appropriately?

5. Are questions simply stated in specific or precise terms?

6. Is there only one question per item?

7. Is there consistency in the way questions are stated and responses are recorded?

8. Do the questions contain slang, ambiguous statements, or educational jargon likely to be misunderstood?

9. Do the questions represent issues that the respondent is familiar with and most likely able to answer?

10. Are questions impersonal and objectively stated?

Observations

Another tool to consider in any program evaluation is that of observation. Although observations take considerable time they provide an excellent opportunity for the evaluators to actually see or experience verification of a behavior, event, or activity under scrutiny. Another advantage of observations as a method for collecting data is the fact that they can be quantitative or qualitative in nature and structured or unstructured in design so that they reflect the intent of the evaluation itself. The structured and quantitative observation involves using formal checklists or standardized forms for recording observations while the qualitative and unstructured observation involves more skill and involvement on the part of the evaluator. Qualitative evaluations can require the evaluator to use one of several strategies for recording information which range from detailed logs or diaries to running notes and anecdotal records. Obviously, observations of either type are more complex and costly when compared to the survey questionnaire approach.

Guidelines for Conducting Observations

1. Consider using a few random observations in conjunction with the survey questionnaires. Often these observations help to clarify common responses from questionnaires or to raise some "red flags" as to inconsistencies from these responses.

2. If you choose to use observations as part of your evaluation plan, begin with quantitative observations which provide evaluators with a checklist of common behaviors or events to look for. This approach acquaints beginning evaluators with the observation method without requiring the degree of skill or training necessary for qualitative observations. Another advantage of quantitative observations is the fact that they do not require as much follow-up time for interpreting findings. Some degree of uniformity and objectivity can be built into this type of observation.

3. If you have experienced evaluators on your evaluation team, however, do try a series of qualitative observations, because they often bring about surprising results and creative ideas. Again, this method can serve as a useful tool for expanding on or explaining selected items from the survey questionnaire.

4. Make certain that whatever type of observation technique is chosen, it is carried out in an unobtrusive manner. The person doing the observation should not interfere with normal routines and activities.

5. The observer should refrain from using either body language (facial expressions or posture clues) or any type of verbal exchanges while conducting an observation. The evaluator is considered to be a "silent visitor" with a mission which is "to be seen and not heard."

Interviews

A third evaluation strategy to consider involves interviews with key stakeholders, clients, and participants. Unlike observers, interviewers can ask probing questions and clarify ambiguous results from items on questionnaires that might otherwise go unexplained. Interviews can be conducted face-to-face or by telephone although both approaches require an experienced interviewer with "scripts" for posing a set of common questions.

Guidelines for Conducting Interviews

1. Use language most commonly understood by the participant. Avoid use of educational jargon.

2. Keep your questions short and to the point. Avoid questions that are so open-ended that responses are likely to be long-winded or ambiguous.

3. Do not assume that the person you are interviewing has a solid knowledge base of factual information on the matter under consideration.

4. Prepare and ask the same set of interview questions to each participant.

5. Record all responses to questions including those that don't seem relevant to the question.

17

6. State all questions in a positive way even though you are asking for reactions/responses with a negative orientation.

7. Don't insult the person you are interviewing in any way. Structure direct questions with right or wrong answers in such a manner that the participant can "save face" if he/she doesn't know the "correct" response.

Self-Checklists

Self-checklists are very simple evaluation tools that provide evaluators with an inventory of single responses from a participant. Checklists are useful if they provide a list in which items can be compared, verified, scheduled, or identified. Such applications, however, are often important if one wants to determine either/or situations that impact on a program component. They are especially useful if done in concert with follow-up observations and/or interviews. The sample instruments in the last section provide the reader with several examples of this correlation of checklists and both observations and interviews.

Guidelines for Developing Checklists

Worthen and Sanders (1987) offer the following guidelines.

1. Use simple, precise language in each of the checklist questions.

2. Make sure questions follow in a logical and effective sequence.

3. Use a positive, nonthreatening tone in phrasing questions.

4. Make questions independent, so answering one does not determine the answer to another.

5. Give coverage in accordance with relative importance of the topic of the question (do not dwell on minor issues and skip over major ones).

6. Group like questions together.

7. Limit scope of question to answerer's probable expertise.

8. Include explanation of purpose of checklist.

9. Make directions unambiguous.

10. Provide instructions for how to fill out and how to turn in, including due date.

Shadow Studies

According to Lounsbury & Johnston (1988), the shadow study supplies realistic snapshots of the educational experiences individuals undergo during an actual school day. By focusing on a randomly selected pupil and the minute-by-minute activities and actions of that pupil, a revealing picture of the educational process is presented. Although the actions of teachers are very much a part of that picture, by looking at the day's events through the eyes of a pupil, a more valid perspective can be secured than when focusing on the teacher's activities alone. When taken together and analyzed, several shadow studies provide a dramatic picture of the real curriculum, the curriculum actually experienced by the individual student.

Guidelines for Conducting Shadow Studies

In following a randomly selected middle grade student, as nearly as possible you will live the school day as he or she does, recording events and impressions. Lounsbury & Johnston (1988) offer the following suggestions.

1. Make prior arrangements with the school to be visited. It is important that teachers understand the purpose of your visit and know that you are not evaluating them.

2. Clear your calendar so that you will be free the entire day to complete the shadow study.

3. Arrive at the school 15 minutes or so ahead of the school opening. Secure or arrange for securing, any basic data needed.

4. Select a student using a technique that will ensure randomness. Do not let school personnel select a "good" student for you. Means of ensuring randomness include:

   a. Ask someone to pick a number between 1 and 25. On the roster of students whose last name begins with your middle initial, select that numbered student.

   b. Locate the file drawer of the student folders and pick, blindly, a folder. (*Note:* if the student selected is in a special education class for more than 25 percent of the day, pick another student.)

5. Locate the selected student's homeroom (or first period) and, with the help of the teacher, unobtrusively identify the student to be shadowed. Find a seat out of the way and look as nonchalant as possible.

6. Record your observations of the student's specific behaviors at 5-7 minute intervals. (See Student Observation Form on next pages. You will need 6-8 copies.) Try to keep your focus on the individual student and what he or she is apparently doing. Use an initial or a fictitious name for the student in recording notes.

7. Go with the student to gym, lunch, and, as nearly as possible, keep up with the individual so you can experience vicariously his or her full school day.

8. If the student confronts you with the question, "Are you following me?" pass it off with a vague statement such as, "You know, I guess you have been in every class I've visited."

9. At the close of the school day, pull the student aside for an interview. You may want to tape record the interview. (See End-of-Day Student Interview Form included.)

10. That evening, if at all possible, write out your impressions, reactions, and conclusions while the day's events are still fresh in your mind.

References:

Lounsbury, J. H., & Johnston, J. H. (1988). *Life in the three sixth grades,* Reston, VA: National Association of Secondary School Principals.

Worthen, B. R. & Sanders, J. R. (1987). *Education evaluation: Alternative approaches and practical guidelines.* New York: Longman.

Student Observation Form

Time	Specific Behavior at 5-7 Minute Intervals	Environment	Impression-Comments

End-of-Day Interview with Student

1. Assume that a new kid moved next door and would be your schoolmate. What are three good things about this school that you would tell him/her?

2. What are three things about this school that you would change, if you could?

3. How do you feel, in general, about your teachers?

4. Is there a person in this school that you would readily turn to for help on a personal problem?

5. How do you feel about the way students treat one another?

6. How do you feel, in general, about your classes? Do they challenge you?

7. Do you have opportunities to help make decisions about what goes on in class?

What Do You Think?

Questions to Consider

1. What are the differences between our school and other schools that should make our evaluation design vary from theirs?

2. What special programs does our school sponsor? What are your most recent, most cutting-edge efforts?

3. What are the main concerns of our students, parents, teachers, staff, and administrators?

4. How much, and what kind of, experience has our school had with evaluation in the past?

5. What forms of evaluation do we think would be most appropriate for our school and why?

6. What advantages/disadvantages does each of the data gathering tools/techniques have for our school setting?

5

How Do You Proceed With Your Customized Evaluation Plan?

Here's What We Think

Although there is no fail-safe method for conducting a successful school evaluation, there are some logical steps to follow in setting up the evaluation design and in completing the evaluation plan. These suggestions should prove helpful in getting the evaluation started.

Step One: Distribute information about the evaluation process to members of the staff and school community. You may want to distribute copies to selected groups or make excerpts available through a series of newsletters, presentations, or information flyers.

Step Two: Organize an evaluation committee or team for your school. Be sure to include representatives from each of the stakeholder groups in the process. Establish a preliminary action plan for meetings, roles, responsibilities, and activities. Determine resources available to the committee in developing and implementing the evaluation plan.

Step Three: Revisit the desired program components of an exemplary middle school program. Decide on those elements of most interest to your team and your stakeholders. Be reasonable in both the number and types of program components you choose to evaluate. Select only those dimensions that are significant to your school population.

Step Four: Determine the major purpose(s) of your evaluation project. Reach consensus as to the types of outcomes you want addressed in the evaluation plan.

Step Five: Review the alternative tools and techniques for evaluating the identified components of your middle level program. Select those that are most appropriate to the goals and objectives of the evaluation process. Allocate resources (time, expertise, dollars, etc.) for conducting the evaluation activities. Formalize the activities through the development of a comprehensive action plan.

Step Six: Select and train the individuals to carry out the varied roles required for the evaluation activities.

Step Seven: Complete the data collecting activities according to the detailed action plan. Make revisions and adjustments to the evaluation plan as needed.

Step Eight: Compile the evaluation results and interpret the evaluation findings from each of the established evaluation activities.

Step Nine: Organize the information into a concise report format. Distribute results to all stakeholders of the evaluation.

Step Ten: Determine ways to use the evaluation results for school improvement.

What Do You Think?

Questions to Consider

1. How will we publicize the need for an evaluation program in our school and community.

2. Who will we select to be on our evaluation committee or team? What evaluation resources can we make available to this committee?

3. What criteria will we use in selecting program components to evaluate?

4. What data do we want to collect and what information do we want to know as a result of our evaluation project?

5. What evaluation tools and techniques will be most appropriate for our evaluation goals and objectives?

6. Who will serve as our data collecting agents and how will they be selected?

7. How flexible can we afford to be in revising our evaluation plan?

8. Who will assume the responsibility for compiling the evaluation results and interpreting the evaluation findings?

9. What format will we use in writing the final evaluation report?

10. How will we know whether any improvement has been made in areas targeted for change based on evaluation results?

6

What Can Be Learned from a Case Study?

Here's What We Think

In order to follow the process for developing a customized evaluation plan, a real life example from a middle level school in the midwestern United States is presented as a case study. It will demonstrate several of the evaluation methods and materials discussed in previous chapters. Because of the confidential nature of the evaluation process, the names, locations, and other particulars have been changed to guarantee anonymity for all involved.

Blue River Middle School, as we'll call it, is in Taft County District 10 with approximately 700 students. Tom Smith, Principal of Blue River, was interested in evaluating several of the middle school practices and programs in his building that had been in operation for two years. He and the staff wanted to conduct a series of formative evaluation activities to determine how close the school was to achieving the quality middle school program identified in the literature.

During the fall of 1990, Tom and his administrative staff gathered information about evaluation tools and procedures that were available to them for conducting a self-study. After collecting and disseminating all the information they could find on the subject, they organized an *Evaluation Steering Committee* who then studied the information collected by the administration on the evaluation process. Attention was also focused on which programs in the school would be evaluated and how they could best be assessed. The programs ultimately selected reflected the main concerns of the school in regard to several of the essential elements implemented as part of the middle school reorganizational plan. It was decided that Taft County District 10 would evaluate the following practices and programs:

1. Advisory Program

2. Interdisciplinary Teams

3. Exploratory Program

4. School/Classroom Discipline

5. School Climate

6. Classroom Instruction

7. Extra-Curricular Offerings

Tools and Techniques Selected

The following tools and techniques were selected for use in collecting data:

1. Surveys to be completed by school personnel, students, and a random sample of parents/guardians touching all of the above programs and practices.

2. Interviews conducted at random with some parents, students, administrators, certified staff, and classified staff touching all of the above areas.

3. Observations of selected classes and team meetings (at least one for each team at each grade level) touching on all of the selected areas.

4. Checklists to be completed by all participants observed from item three above in the areas of Advisory, Interdisciplinary Teaming, and Instruction.

These methods of evaluation provided both the flexibility and the desired ownership associated with the informal evaluation process. Each of the instruments was accompanied by directions and a clarification of the circumstances under which it was to be used. (Sample evaluation instruments are included in the last section.) The checklists, observations, and interviews with teachers were all coordinated to solicit the same types of information from those who engaged in the activities.

An Evaluation Team Selected

The Evaluation Steering Committee then organized an Evaluation Team of in-house evaluators to administer the surveys, conduct the interviews and observations, and compile/interpret the results. The Evaluation Team was composed of two administrators and one teacher from each grade level. The team was briefed on the procedures for administering surveys and for conducting observations and interviews. An additional team member was added from the School District Office upon completion of all data collection activities for purposes of compiling and interpreting the statistical information. This person was skilled in the areas of statistics, research, and technology.

The final report was written collaboratively by all six members of the Evaluation Team and shared with the various groups of stakeholders in the school setting and community. Decisions for changing or improving existing programs were then made based on the evaluation results. According to Principal Smith, this informal, self-study approach to evaluating their school was highly successful because decisions in developing the evaluation design, in implementing the evaluation activities, and in interpreting the evaluation results were made in-house by those who were closest to the situation and had the most to gain from the experience.

Because the information was to be used locally to improve their school, few people were intimidated by or resistant to the evaluation results. Tom Smith summarized it all when he stated that "we learned as much about ourselves from the evaluation process as we did from the evaluation report." When asked what he and the Evaluation Steering Committee might do differently next time, Tom indicated that he would definitely want to add the dimension of shadow studies to the evaluation design because of the additional insights it would provide his stakeholders.

What Do You Think?

Questions to Consider

1. How should we select members to serve on our Evaluation Steering Committee and how should we organize their tasks and responsibilities?

2. How should we determine membership on the Evaluation Team?

3. What type of training do we need to provide members of the Evaluation Team and who would deliver it?

4. Which of the evaluation tools and techniques do we think would provide our school with the best information for improving programs already in place?

5. To what degree do we want to involve central office personnel in our evaluation process? What roles, if any, should they play? What are the advantages and disadvantages of using central office personnel?

6. Do we want to use technology as part of the evaluation design, and are we able to do so?

7. How should we disseminate the results of the evaluation to stakeholders, the school community, and others?

How Can Technology Be Used As an Evaluation Tool?

Here's What We Think

All mass surveys administered as part of the evaluation process ought to be technology driven. So much more information can be compiled and interpreted through computer software designed for evaluation purposes. These programs will permit you to use quantitative data to make more qualitative decisions than would otherwise be possible. For example, while a median or average statistic has some value, it fails to adequately represent the range of responses often essential in making intelligent decisions relating to a program. We need to avoid the false security that may result when only looking at a single generalized response. The views of a significant minority too often get lost in the assessment process only to surface later as the vocal majority.

The following paragraphs provide an example of how technology was used in the Case Study of Blue River Middle School. It is a continuation of the evaluation process used by this real school (only name and location changed) and is presented with examples of the types of data that were derived from the simple surveys when technology was applied.

From Raw Data to Printout:

After the programs to be evaluated and the instruments to be used were determined, the Evaluation Team proceeded to administer the surveys, perform the observations, and conduct the interviews. Next, appropriate members of the Evaluation Team tabluated the numerical data and interpreted the non-statistical data. As part of this process, the returned questionnaires, filled-in bubble sheets, and completed surveys were keyed into a computerized system for analysis and broken down into appropriate categories (respondent and question number). The tabulated results yielded totals, means, standard deviations, and other statistical indicators of meaning.

Bubble-sheets were scanned (using scan-tron sheets) and results were printed out from their computer-ready form. After all used instruments had been reduced to computer format, the originals were stored until the evaluation results were compiled and the project completed. Until then, originals might be needed for consultation. For safety purposes, raw data printouts were also kept and stored until the project was over. Floppy-discs and other electronic/magnetic means of storage can prove to be insufficient safeguards for information laboriously gathered.

The most difficult task for the Evaluation Team was to *interpret* these raw data so that informed and helpful decisions could be made, decisions that would lead to real improvement.

From Printout to Inspecting Variables

On the first page of the printout from the Blue River Middle School Evaluation, the following information appeared:

Variable	Label	N	NMISS	MEAN	STD DEV	MIN	MAX	STD ERR	CV
BSICSKIL	Basic Skills	509	5	1.8251	0.9469	1.0000	5.000	0.042	51.878

The column "VARIABLE" shows the codes used to label the variables. Variables are the items of information about the responders or the responses which are subject to several options, such as "teacher" and "student," or "strongly agree" and "strongly disagree." A code or series of letters was assigned to each variable so that the computer could best present the information in tabular form. While examining a table, one can refer to "LABEL" to identify which variable a code represented.

The column "N" shows the number of individuals who responded to each inquiry; some respondents will always leave a few questions blank or answer improperly, and their responses cannot be included in the statistical consideration. The column "NMISS" shows this value.

The remaining columns show results from statistical manipulation of the information for each variable (question or issue receiving a response). They are:

MEAN ———— mean
STD DEV ——— standard deviation
MINIMUM——— minimum value
MAXIMUM —— maximum value
STD ERROR — standard error of mean
CV ———————— coefficient of variation

With information of this kind, one has the results from each question or inquiry, indicating the most frequent response, the average response, how many people responded, how many people didn't respond, and the level of variation among the responses (how much they varied).

Even more useful to the Evaluation Team was the information put into tabular form or *cross-tabulation* which shows exactly how many of each respondent category answered in a particular way. The cross-tabulation compares one variable aspect of a responder or response to another, yielding a further dimension of information.

FREQUENCY PERCENT ROW PCT COL PCT	STRONGLY AGREE	AGREE	NEUTRAL	DIS-AGREE	STRONGLY DISAGREE	TOTAL
STUDENT	61.00	229.00	137.00	32.00	11.00	470.00
	11.03	41.41	24.77	5.79	1.99	84.99
	12.98	48.72	29.15	6.81	2.34	
	91.04	84.19	86.16	78.05	78.57	
CORE TCHR	1.00	13.00	7.00	4.00	1.00	26.00
	.18	2.35	1.27	.72	.18	4.70
	3.85	50.00	26.92	15.38	3.85	
	1.49	4.78	4.40	9.76	7.14	
EXPLOR/ ELEC	1.00	7.00	2.00	0.00	0.00	10.00
	.18	1.27	.36	0.00	0.00	1.81
	10.00	70.00	20.00	0.00	0.00	
	1.49	2.57	1.26	0.00	0.00	
PARENT/ GUARD	1.00	12.00	4.00	3.00	0.00	20.00
	.18	2.17	.72	.54	0.00	3.62
	5.00	60.00	20.00	15.00	0.00	
	1.49	4.41	2.52	7.32	0.00	
ADMINIS	0.00	2.00	1.00	0.00	0.00	3.00
	0.00	.36	.18	0.00	0.00	.54
	0.00	66.67	33.33	0.00	0.00	
	0.00	.74	.63	0.00	0.00	
SUPPORT STAFF/CE	1.00	2.00	2.00	0.00	2.00	7.00
	.18	.36	.36	0.00	.36	1.27
	14.29	28.57	28.57	0.00	28.57	
	1.49	.74	1.26	0.00	14.29	
SUPPORT STAFF/CL	2.00	7.00	6.00	2.00	0.00	17.00
	.36	1.27	1.08	.36	0.00	3.07
	11.76	41.18	35.29	11.76	0.00	
	2.99	2.57	3.77	4.88	0.00	
TOTAL	67.00	272.00	159.00	41.00	14.00	553.00
	12.12	49.19	28.75	7.41	2.53	100.00

From Inspecting Variables to Measures

The usefulness and meaningfulness of data compiled depends entirely on the extent to which the information is interpreted fully and correctly. One may be reluctant to deal with the terms and mathematics involved, but it is well worth the effort to draw upon previous experience in measurement or to call upon qualified personnel for assistance. The following is in no way intended to be a sufficient introduction to the important statistical issues. For more information, a standard text on educational evaluation should be consulted.

Most statistical interpretations try to show relationships between the responses on a particular item. Beginning with the average (mean) and range of responses (highest and lowest, or maximum and minimum values), more sophisticated measures show how much answers varied among each other and how much they varied from the average (averages of differences from the average). One of the most useful measures, the *standard deviation,* functions as a unit of measurement for a particular response based on how much all responses differed from one another in relation to the average (mean).

Significance or "The Big Picture"

The standard deviation is large if the differences (*variance*) among responses are great; it is small if the differences are minor. A diffused response may indicate a general lack of certainty on the part of the respondents; a fairly unanimous response may show stronger assurance. The interpreter of data must take the known, the observed, and the context into account to explain the results. *Tables of significance* should also be used to see whether there is a significant preference for one response over another.

In the illustration below, out of 509 students who responded (N), not counting blanks or multiple answers from the 514 total, the majority (mean) answered favorably for the following on "BASIC SKILLS."

I have an opportunity to learn the basic skills at my school. (math facts, reading, etc.)

This is labeled BSICSKIL or BASIC SKILLS. The options were:

1 — strongly agree
2 — agree
3 — neither agree nor disagree
4 — disagree
5 — strongly disagree

Variable	Label	N	NMI SS	MEAN	STD DEV	MIN	MAX	STD ERR	CV
BSICSKIL	Basic Skills	509	5	1.8251	0.9469	1.0000	5.000	0.042	51.878

The numbers one through five are the range of options, of which 1.8251 was found to be the mean for students' response to this item. This is favorable because 1.8251 places it between "strongly agree" and "agree"; it was one of the strongest responses in the survey. The mean alone, however, will give only a partial idea of the variety of response. The standard deviation shows the variation among responses. If the standard deviation had been large, it would have indicated a more dispersed response, one which might have indicated that a significant number of students had disagreed. In this case, the standard deviation was 0.9469, which is low enough to indicate the positive response was representative of the strong majority.

Minimum and maximum designations show the range of responses, which are generally the highest and lowest values available, in this case "1" and "5." The standard error 0.042 for this item was low and the coefficient of variation was 51.878 which further reinforces the positive interpretation.

Another item was:

I am pleased with the advisory activities in this school.

This time the response, shown in the figures below, was favorable again, with a mean of 2.378 putting it with an average response of between "agree" and "neither agree nor disagree" but closer to "agree," as the low standard error demonstrates. The high standard deviation shows that there was a wide variety of responses, although the total numbers made the results the way they are (the coefficient of variation shows relationship of the standard deviation to the mean).

Variable	Label	N	NMISS	MEAN	STD DEV	MIN	MAX	STD ERR	CV
HBSEAC	ADV	508.6	6	2.3780	1.2667	1.0000	5.000	0..0562	53.2664

What Do You Think?

Questions to Consider

1. What kinds of evaluation instruments have been chosen? What kind of data do they provide? What kinds of questions are they best suited to answer?

2. How will we provide for the collection of evaluation data? Where will the hard copy be stored after it is downloaded electronically? Who will enter the information into the computer?

3. Who will conduct the statistical analysis of the data? What and who are our resources for interpreting statistical data?

4. Based on statistical analysis, do responses show much divergence or unanimity on each item? Is one response on a particular item chosen significantly more often than others?

5. Based on our observation and first-hand knowledge, is there more than one possible reason for the results we obtained?

8

How Should the Evaluation Report Be Written?

Here's What We Think

When deciding on the types of information to include in the report and the best format to use in presenting it, several critical questions must be addressed. These include:

1. What is the purpose of the data report?
2. Who will be the target audience(s) of the final report?
3. What data will be most important to those audiences?
4. What is the best format for the data? How should the page/sections look?
5. How do we want the data organized or sorted? Ranked? Compared?
6. When and where will the data be analyzed?
7. How much of the data can be handled through technology?

Once the answers to these questions have been determined, a school has a set of parameters within which it can design the report. The following paragraphs present possible sections that might be in a final report. A condensed sample for each of the sections also follows.

1. **The State of the Art** provides a synthesis of the professional literature on the essential elements of an exemplary middle school. It can serve as a reminder, checklist, or comparative "shopping list" for comparing the ideal middle school with the school being evaluated.

2. **Analysis of the Survey Data** provides a summary of the information gathered as part of the widespread surveys administered to various groups i.e. students, faculty, administrators, parents/guardians, and support staff.

3. **Commendations and Recommendations** contains a synthesis of the results from checklists, interviews, and observations. It summarizes the findings from all target populations into a manageable format for making school improvement decisions.

4. **Rationale Statements for Selected Recommendations** can be very important when it comes to supporting the recommendations. Very often stakeholders need to be convinced of the need for change and documentation from quality research efforts and informed judgments from the literature can be very convincing in such situations.

5. **Evaluation Instrument** contains copies of all the tools used in the evaluation process. Readers of the report should have access to the questions, topics, procedures, and conditions for clarification and validation purposes.

6. **Where To Go for More Detailed Information** is important as a bibliography for schools wishing to locate more data and informed opinion from the literature to document essential elements of effective middle level schools.

What Do You Think?

Questions to Consider

1. What characteristics of exemplary schools will we include in our "State of the Art" section?

2. What are the high and low points of both the quantitative and qualitative dimensions produced as part of our evaluation results?

3. Based on the evaluation results, what school specific commendations and recommendations seem to be appropriate? What are the specific strengths and weaknesses of our school as indicated by the evaluation results?

4. What authoritative sources of information should we cite from the literature to document the specific recommendations made?

5. What practical steps might our school take toward strengthening the areas that have been determined to be less than satisfactory? How will the strengths of our school program be communicated to and celebrated by the stakeholders involved?

The State of the Art

Blue River Middle School

The essential elements of an effective middle school include the following:

1. a philosophy based on the unique needs of early adolescents

2. educators knowledgeable about and committed to young adolescents

3. a balanced curriculum between the cognitive and affective needs of young adolescents

4. teachers who use varied instructional strategies

5. a full exploratory program

6. a comprehensive advisor/advisee program

7. interdisciplinary team organization at all grades

8. a flexible block master schedule

9. team planning and personal planning for all teachers

10. a positive school climate

11. shared decision making where the people closest to the "client" are involved in the decision making process of the school

12. a smooth transition process from elementary to middle school and from middle school to high school

13. principals who are knowledgeable about and committed to the middle school philosophy, programs, and practices

14. a strong co-curricular program including intramurals, interest based mini-courses, clubs, and periodic social events

15. a physical plant in which teams can be housed together for core classes and in which there are large areas for full teams to meet

16. a commitment to the importance of health and physical fitness for all students on a regular basis

17. a commitment to reengage families in the education of young adolescents by keeping them informed of student progress and school programs and by giving them meaningful roles in the schooling process

18. a connection between school and the community through student service projects, business partnerships, and the use of community resources inside the school

19. use of cooperative learning strategies in the classroom

20. an emphasis on developing higher order thinking skills and hands-on instructional strategies.

The twenty characteristics of exemplary middle schools were derived from an examination of the following sources:

The exemplary middle school. (1981). Alexander, W. & George, P. New York: Holt Rinehart & Winston.

Turning points: Preparing American youth for the 21st century. (1989). Carnegie Council on Adolescent Development. New York: Carnegie Corporation of New York.

This we believe. (1992). Columbus, OH: National Middle School Association.

An agenda for excellence at the middle level. (1985). Reston, VA: National Association of Secondary School Principals.

Interviews, observations, visitations, and research studies compiled by the National Resource Center for Middle Grades Education at the University of South Florida.

Analysis of the Survey Data
Blue River Middle School

A. Explanation of the Reports Produced

This was generally a descriptive analysis of several different surveys given to varied client populations within the school. The client populations included: students, faculty, counselor(s), administrator(s), parents/guardians, and support staff. Approximately thirty-three interval scale questions were asked with five options from strongly agree to strongly disagree for responses. Where numerical results are presented (including the statistics of means, etc.), it is important to remember that low numbers mean higher levels of agreement with a positively worded survey item. In the current reports and analyses, we have restricted our procedures to those which convey the information in its simplest and yet most powerful forms.

Two basic summary report forms were chosen. The first is a report which provides basic descriptive statistics on each question, including the relevant means of the questions, grouping means of questions, and certain other descriptors (variables) all on one page. The second report is a cross-tabulation or tables report which compares any two questions or variables. A great deal of care was taken in selecting variable names and descriptors which would allow the computer printed reports to be usable by the several different client groups. These are briefly summarized below.

Variable Name/Descriptors for Report One

1. VARIABLE, the name of the variable.
2. LABEL, the descriptive label attached to the variable name in most of the different reports provided.
3. N, the number of nonmissing values for the variable (the remaining statistics all just use the nonmissing values for their calculations).
   3a. NMISS (not printed on all analyses), the number of missing values for the variable (the remaining statistics did not use these cases for this variable). Questions which were not asked of all client populations would include missing values for all the client populations for which the questions had not been asked.
4. MEAN or average of the nonmissing values for the variable.
5. STANDARD DEVIATION (STD DEV) of the variable, or a measure of dispersion from the mean in terms of the units of the original data. It is computed by taking the square root of the variance. The higher the standard deviation, the greater the disagreement among the respondents on their responses to the questions.
6. MINIMUM VALUE of the variable (lowest value of all respondents), which gives an idea of the range of responses.
7. MAXIMUM VALUE of the variable (highest value of all respondents), the second part of the range of responses.

Some reports do not contain the following additional statistics which though helpful to some readers may be more than are required by most readers.

8. STD ERROR (OF MEAN), the standard error of the mean, a measure of the precision of the mean, computed by dividing the standard deviation by the square root of the N (number of nonmissing values).

9. C.V. or the coefficient of variation (the standard deviation divided by the mean) is expressed as a percentage and is found on some forms of this report that do not include the variable LABEL.

Variable Name/Descriptors for Report Two

The cross-tabulation or tables report compares any two variables.

1. Variable Name (e.g., ACOPP, with its associated label "Academic Opportunity") for the variable on the vertical part of the table (right side, up and down or vertical)

2. Variable Name (e.g., CLIENT with its associated label "Classification of Respondent") for the variable on the horizontal (top, left to right) part of the table

3. FREQUENCY counts, giving the number of subjects that have the indicated values of the two variables

4. PERCENT, the percentage of the total frequency count represented by that cell

5. ROW PCT, or the row percentage, the percent of the total frequency count for that row represented by the cell

6. COL PCT, or the column percent, the percent of the total frequency count for that column represented by the cell

Other reports provided include the following: a number of simple graphic analyses of the client populations and/or some of the summary variables and, at the district level, some strength of relationship analyses provided to district staff.

B. Grouping Variables Developed

Several variables were created by taking the mean of the nonmissing values of other variables. One of these variables was the mean of all the survey questions which asked for a judgment based upon the uniform scale (MEANSURV). Other grouping or summary variables attempt to summarize a basic concept which was the focus of the survey. These variables were the means of other survey questions which were deemed to be similar. Those mean variables were academic (ACADEMIC), discipline (DISCIPLN), involvement in the master schedule (IN-VOLVES), input into the decision process, "control" or involvement (INVOLVEG), adult interaction (INTERACT), social/emotional needs (SOCEMOT), and a junior high/middle school philosophy (JRMIDDLE) variable.

Students provided the largest number of surveys completed. Any grouping of the client populations without weighing different client groups would give the majority of weight to the student responses. Therefore the executive summary which groups all the populations as one group has certain distortions associated with any summary. A summary of the individual client populations is also provided so that a more detailed view of the middle school client populations might be available. Differences between the responses of these groups and the population taken as a single group might be great but was not specifically noted in the highlights. It was also difficult to use some of the more powerful summary statistics to examine the differences between the groups because of the small size of most of the client groups. Proper weighing might solve some of these problems but that would require the researcher to work more closely with the district staff and make certain assumptions based upon district level judgments about the proper weighing of the several client population responses. However, client groups with populations above fifteen were generally examined for important and material differences with the grand mean(s) results reported below.

The careful manner in which the parent/client population was sampled and coded by the district staff could lend itself to further detailed analysis. The population size was estimated and the sample size selected to allow for a certain statistically defined prediction probability for the instrument to measure the feelings of parent population as a whole. The sample was selected and rigorous methods were used to obtain responses from all the members of the sample population. District staff were able to obtain responses from all of the sample parents by using aggressive follow-up techniques. Further work here could certainly provide a wealth of additional information if desired because of the careful planning of the district staff.

Certain judgments might best be made by examining the responses of individual or other component client population groupings. A "Basic Descriptive Statistics" report has been provided for each of the individual client populations.

C. Highlights of Survey Results

At Blue River Middle School the satisfaction level of all the respondent groups taken as a single group was above the midpoint of the range as expressed by the mean of the survey variable, MEANSURV, at 2.62 (1 would be the highest, 5 the lowest given the positive wording of the questions, the mean being 3) with a standard deviation of only .64. The lowest component mean was discipline as summarized by the variable DISCIPLN, discipline mean, which was 3.11 with a standard deviation of .82. The other component summary variables were the mean of the control items, INVOLVEG, with a mean of 2.80 and the schedule involvement mean, INVOLVES, with a mean 2.69 and a standard deviation of 1.17. The variable ACADEMIC, mean of the academic items, was reasonably high at 2.17 (SD=.83). The middle school philosophy seemed to be favored with a mean of 2.56 (SD=1.20) (JRMIDDLE variable). The social/emotional needs variable, SOCEMOT, had a mean of 2.84. Adult interactions (INTERACT) had a mean of 2.22 (SD=.82). The several client groups seemed to see most of the areas in the same way.

Commendations and Recommendations

Blue River Middle School

Commendations

1. It is apparent that the faculty and staff at Blue Lake Middle School enjoy working together and that they feel a part of the school.

2. The basic skills education program is perceived as being strong.

3. There is clear evidence of interdisciplinary instruction at Blue Lake Middle School.

4. The level of sophistication of instruction was in evidence on a number of occasions. For example, the Cheetah team was discussing their use of Bloom's Taxonomy during a team meeting. This is emphasized regularly in this team.

5. The special education model is excellent. The consult/collaborative model is in place *and* special education teachers and their students are on core teams.

6. The alteration of the homebase program structure, district wide, at the semester break is definitely a step in the right direction. Now, the number of students in homebase is much lower and all teachers are taking part in a very important program.

7. The streamlining of teaming at grade 8 is excellent. There are only four teachers who must cross-team. This is a definite step in the right direction.

8. The teams are strong at Blue Lake Middle School.

9. The club activities at the end of the day on Fridays are excellent.

10. The smaller teams at grade 6 make for an excellent transition from elementary to middle school.

11. A very creative use of teaming is evidenced when two grade level teams cross-team briefly for remediation and enrichment purposes.

12. Student work is displayed in the halls. This feature helps create a positive student climate.

13. The counselors meet at least once per week with their teams.

14. There is evidence of excellent instruction at Blue Lake Middle School. The evaluator witnessed some good "hands-on" instruction taking place.

15. There is a definite commitment to interdisciplinary instruction at Blue Lake Middle School.

Recommendations

1. Teams should strengthen the team identity through the acquisition and use of team names, slogans, banners, full team meetings, and other outward signs of unity and identity.

2. The exploratory teachers should be given a common planning time if at all possible. They need to feel the sense of belonging to a team of their own.

3. Teachers need to have more flexibility with regard to the activities used during homebase. The curriculum is excellent. The choices of activities now need to be team-centered to allow for more ownership and creativity.

4. The extra-curricular program needs strengthening. There is *very* little opportunity for students to be involved in clubs, intramurals, or other "extra" events.

5. The advisory period is of *minimum* length. To further strengthen the program, perhaps additional time could be added next fall.

6. The advisory program needs a name and identity.

7. Although full teaming at grade 8 has *almost* been accomplished, efforts should be made to eliminate cross-teaming altogether if possible.

8. It is evident from the computer printouts and interviews that discipline is a concern. This issue needs to be addressed.

9. Teams should work on strengthening the integration of curriculum through activities such as conducting interdisciplinary units, having common team vocabulary, having a team skill of the week, etc.

10. It appears that a fair amount of faculty and staff still question the effectiveness of the advisory program. This issue also needs to be addressed.

Rationale Statements for Selected Recommendations

Blue River Middle School

1. *Teaming at Grade 8*

All students in a middle school need to feel a sense of belonging to a group. When only certain grade levels are teamed and others are not, that sense of belonging is diminished. In addition, some faculty members are also denied that same sense of belonging and are unable to take full advantage of the benefits of teaming such as coordinating instruction, a block schedule, meeting with students as a team, conducting team parent conferences, and meeting on a daily basis to discuss common concerns.

2. *The Structure of Special Education*

When a school is organized into teams and special education students are pulled out of their teams into a departmentalized situation, the ultimate loser is the child. We must do all we can within the structure to service all students within their home team. The collaborative/inclusion model of special education is a model which involves placing special education teachers on core teams where they collaborate with "regular" teachers and service students within the team. The ultimate winners in this model are the students.

3. *Team Leader Council*

In order for shared decision-making to be effective in a team structure team leaders should meet on a regular basis with the administrative team. This Team Leader Council assists with school-wide decisions and helps keep communication lines open and working.

4. *Team Identity*

In order for students to gain a strong sense of belonging to a particular group, that group should have a distinctive name and outward signs of that identity. Early adolescents are still, for the most part, in Piaget's concrete operational stage. Concrete signs of belonging can be powerful tools to enhance team affiliation and strengthen commitment to a group.

5. *Counselors Meeting With Teams*

Counselors should be assigned to teams and should meet with teams on a regular basis to discuss particular students, assist in team decisions, and report results back to the teams. The team structure enhances the counseling process since counselors are able to meet with all core teachers at one time.

6. *The Exploratory Team*

In many middle schools, exploratory teachers feel like second class citizens. When only academic teachers are organized into teams and emphasis is placed on the teaming structure to enhance the sense of belonging for students and core teachers, exploratory teachers are not afforded that same sense of support and collaboration. By contrast, when the exploratory teachers are organized so that they become a team and are attached to core teams via the advisory program, teacher morale and that sense of truly belonging are enhanced for everyone. In addition, exploratory teachers are then able to communicate on a regular basis, correlate and integrate their curriculum, discuss students, and encourage one another.

7. *Teams and Discipline*

The very best teams "skin their own skunks." Effective teams do *not* give up power and control by sending students with discipline difficulties to the office. Instead, they devise creative methods to handle problems within the team structure and only ask for office assistance when absolutely necessary.

8. *Co-curricular Programs*

Effective middle level programs provide additional activities for students before and after school hours. In the age of two working families and/or working single parent families, students need to have opportunities to be involved in meaningful activities such as drama, sports, intramurals, and clubs so that their extra time is spent expanding horizons in a positive and supervised situation. Co-curricular programs are also major means of fulfilling the exploratory responsibility of the school.

9. *Alternative Instructional Strategies*

Middle grades students learn best "with their mouths open and their hands on." Therefore, it is *not* appropriate to use lecture or direct instruction as the main instructional tool. Middle grades teachers must be taught alternative strategies such as cooperative learning, learning centers, simulations, role-playing, and incorporation of thinking skills into the curriculum.

10. *Advisory Class Length*

In order to carry out most recommended advisory activities and accomplish additional "housekeeping" responsibilities, the literature recommends a daily period of 25-30 minutes.

11. *Advisory Activities*

In order for advisory activities to be effective, teachers must be able to pick and choose activities appropriate to them and their students. A complete manual should be provided which includes more than enough activities required in a given month. Then, individual teachers and/ or teams can choose appropriate activities. People support what they help create and choice must be provided.

12. *A Name for the Advisory Program*

Just as teams must have strong team identity through team names, logos, slogans, and tee shirts, the National Resource Center for Middle Grades Education recommends that the advisory program have a set of symbols which identifies as well as explains the focus of the program. You might also consider creating a logo, slogan, or club to enhance the name and promote the importance of advisory time as an integral part of the curriculum.

13. *Integration of Curriculum*

The world is integrated and subjects are indeed interrelated. A team of teachers with different subject matter specialties must work together to show students how these subjects connect. In fact, numerous studies show that students learn better when they can see these connections and when subject matter is approached through conceptual themes rather than by isolated subjects. In addition, when teachers are shown how to effectively integrate subject matter, there is often a renewed enthusiasm for teaching which becomes contagious.

14. *Flexible Block Schedule*

Life outside of school does *not* rotate around 45 minute periods. Teachers must take advantage of a block of time and use it to better meet the needs of their students by altering the time allotments. If a science teacher on a team needs 75 minutes for a science lab experience, the block of time can be and should be altered to meet for this need.

15. *Advisory Placement Within Schedule*

Upon observing numerous advisory programs and interviewing personnel, the Resource Center recommends placing advisory at the beginning of the school day and, if at all possible, allowing time for students to *briefly* revisit the homebase teacher at the end of the day. The morning placement allows students to begin their day on a positive note with their adult advocate and allows that adult advocate to speak with other team members if a child is experiencing any difficulties which may carry over into the day. The end of the day contact allows the advocate to touch base with students and remind them of evening responsibilities.

Where To Go for More Detailed Information

Blue River Middle School

The following section is to be used as an addendum to the Middle Grades Evaluation Project for Blue River Middle School, Taft County District 10. The sources cited here contain material which helps substantiate the *recommendations* made. To use this document, the reader is asked to turn to the original recommendations as stated in the full report. References are included here which provide background for the recommendations.

1. **Advisory**

Beane, J. A. (1990). *Affect in the curriculum: Toward democracy, dignity, and diversity.* New York: Teachers College, Columbia University.

Beane, J. A. & Lipka, R. P. (1987). *When the kids come first: Enhancing self-esteem.* Columbus, OH: National Middle School Association.

Cole, C. G. (1992). *Nurturing a teacher advisory program.* Columbus, OH: National Middle School Association.

James, M. (1986). *Advisor-advisee programs: Why, what and how.* Columbus, OH: National Middle School Association.

2. **Curriculum and Instruction**

Beane, J. A. (1990). *A middle school curriculum: From rhetoric to reality.* Columbus, OH: National Middle School Association.

Callahan, J. F., Clark, L. H., & Kellough, R. D. (1992). *Teaching in the middle and secondary schools.* New York: Macmillan.

Jacobs, H. H., (Ed.) (1989). *Interdisciplinary curriculum: Design and implementation.* Alexandria, VA: Association for Supervision and Curriculum Development.

Ornstein, A. C. (1992). *Secondary and middle school teaching methods.* New York: HarperCollins.

3. **Discipline**

Curwin, R. L. & Mendler, A. N. (1988). *Discipline with dignity.* Alexandria, VA: Association for Supervision and Curriculum Development.

Purkey, W. W. & Strahan, D. B. (1986). *Positive discipline: A pocketful of ideas.* Columbus, OH: National Middle School Association.

4. Exploratory/Extracurricular Programs

Garvin, J. P. (1989). *Merging the exploratory and basic subjects in the middle level school: Practical suggestions that work.* Rowley, MA: New England League of Middle Schools.

5. Interdisciplinary Teaming

Erb, T. O. & Doda, N. M. (1989). *Team organization: Promise — practices and possibilities.* Washington, D.C.: National Education Association.

Merenbloom, E. Y. (1991). *The team process: A handbook for teachers.* Columbus, OH: National Middle School Association.

Vars, Gordon F. (1987). *Interdisciplinary teaching in the middle grades.* Columbus, OH: National Middle School Association.

6. Middle School Organizational Pattern

Alexander, W. M. & George P. S. (1981). *The exemplary middle school.* New York: Holt, Rinehart and Winston.

Alexander, W. M. & McEwin, C. K. (1989). *Schools in the middle: Status and progress.* Columbus, OH: National Middle School Association.

Capelluti, J. & Stokes, D. (1991). *Middle level education: Policies, programs, and practices.* Reston, VA: National Association of Secondary School Principals.

Carnegie Council on Adolescent Development. Task Force on Education of Young Adolescents. *Turning points: Preparing American youth for the 21st century:* New York: Carnegie Council of New York.

Eichhorn, D. H. (1987). *The middle school.* Columbus, OH: National Middle School Association.

Epstein, J. & Mac Iver, D. (1990). *Education in the middle grades: National practices and trends.* Columbus, OH: National Middle School Association.

George, P. & Lawrence, G. (1982). *Handbook for middle school teaching.* Glenview, IL: Scott, Foresman.

George, P. S., Stevenson, C., Thomason, J., & Beane, J. (1992). *The middle school — and beyond.* Alexandria, VA: Association for Supervision and Curriculum Development.

Irvin, J. L.(Ed.). (1992). *Transforming middle level education: Perspectives and possibilities.* Boston: Allyn and Bacon.

Lipsitz, J. (1984). *Successful schools for young adolescents.* New Brunswick, NJ: Transaction.

National Association of Secondary School Principals' Council on Middle Level Education. (1989). *Middle level education's responsibility for intellectual development.* Reston, VA: National Association of Secondary School Principals.

National Association of Secondary School Principals' Council on Middle Level Education. (1988). *Assessing excellence: A guide for studying the middle level school.* Reston, VA: National Association of Secondary School Principals.

National Association of Secondary School Principals' Council on Middle Level Education. (1987). *Developing a mission statement for the middle level school.* Reston, VA: National Association of Secondary School Principals.

National Association of Secondary School Principals' Council on Middle Level Education. (1985). *An agenda for excellence at the middle level.* Reston, VA: National Association of Secondary School Principals.

Wiles, J. & Bondi, J. (1986). *Making middle schools work.* Alexandria, VA: Association for Supervision and Curriculum Development.

9

How Can We Make Good Use of the Evaluation Results?

Here's What We Think

After completing the final Evaluation Report, the question remains, what should we do with the information? Because the evaluation project should have been part of an overall school improvement plan, the evaluation can function as a valid and pertinent basis for school improvement efforts. As part of an ongoing process, the evaluation must not function "to conclude" but rather "to instigate" action. Evaluation findings certainly should guide long-term and day-to-day decisions.

To begin with, the results of the evaluation ought to be disseminated as broadly as possible to those who participated and have a stake in the evaluation process and its results. Receiving the results will confirm ownership and raise the awareness of all about the school's progress.

The evaluation will clarify the gap between the status and the goals established as well as the vision contained in the state of the art, exemplary school. Those gaps, the discrepancies between "where we are" and "where we want to be" should be used to motivate students, staff, and community in support of the school's improvement strategies. Improvement goals will thus be clear challenges, yet achievable ones.

The resulting action plan must include strategies tailored for addressing the problems with needed personnel and resources and plans for evaluating outcomes. By developing an informal self-evaluation plan, the school has accepted responsibility for progress towards its own goals. By making frequent reports of progress, the school provides essential feedback to all stakeholders associated with the school and lets them know that the evaluation project was not shelved.

In order for the school stakeholders to take action, the school must support risk-taking and reward innovation, as well as empower staff to take action. The school must also take an open approach to means of organizing personnel and allowing reasonable time for results to surface.

Another consideration to keep in mind is that professional development is the key to ensuring effective progress toward goals. The evaluation instruments themselves raise awareness of school issues and priorities and special training in evaluation benefits the entire school.

Finally, the evaluation should be an integral part of a continuous cycle of change and improvement, so that the momentum gained by one step will fuel progress toward the next step. In such a way, one's school can be assured of coming closer and closer to its own predetermined vision.

What Do You Think?

Questions to Consider

1. In what ways do the evaluation criteria relate to our school's vision?

2. What is the next step in our school improvement, long-term plan? Under which circumstances will another evaluation monitor the progress made since the last evaluation?

3. What needs has our school evaluation revealed? What specific, concrete actions and strategies would address these needs?

4. Who will bear the responsibility for actions taken and how will those roles be defined and communicated? What resources will be provided? What staff development options would be appropriate?

A Sampler of Evaluation Instruments

The following collection includes some of the instruments used to evaluate Blue River Middle School. They are presented as suggestions and/or models to be used in designing various tools and techniques for conducting a middle school self-evaluation.

The sampler contains a variety of instruments — surveys, checklists, and interview questions — which can be used to solicit the opinions and impressions of various groups and individuals. Results from these surveys (pages 67- 78) are capable of strict quantitative manipulation; the checklists and interview answers can be evaluated by more informal weightings. Each of the instruments provides a particular insight into the state of the school's programs. Any instrument developed should be done conscientiously and carefully with every consideration given to the ultimate purpose and scope of the evaluation itself.

The first set of sample instruments presented is on teaming: a checklist for the team, an observation form for the team meeting, and an interview form for the team member. The next set is for evaluating the teacher advisory program: a teacher self-checklist, an advisory class observation form, and a teacher interview form. For classroom evaluation, the sample set of instruments contains a teacher checklist, a teacher observation form, and a teacher interview form. Following this is a set of open-ended interview questions.

The special set of surveys which follows has one set of directions, whether the respondent is student, teacher, parent, administrator, or support staff. Each respondent receives the same set of directions with the survey appropriate to his or her classification as teacher, parent, etc. A special letter to accompany the parent/guardian survey is also included.

Team Effectiveness Instrument

Part One

The Team Self-Checklist

This checklist should be completed individually by all members of an interdisciplinary team prior to a designated team meeting. Then, the team leader should facilitate a meeting where responses are shared and consensus is reached. The agreed upon answers should be recorded on a master sheet, kept in the team notebook, and reviewed on a regular basis.

	Always	Frequently	Infrequently	Never	Comments
1. Our team meets on a regular basis.					
2. All team members are present at our team meetings.					
3. All team members come to our meetings on time.					
4. All team members stay for the duration of meetings.					
5. Our team discusses ways to best meet student needs.					
6. Our team works effectively with resource personnel, such as our counselor and our house leader.					
7. Team members support the efforts of our team leader.					
8. Every member of our team participates in the decision making process.					
9. The team decisions are implemented.					
10. Our team keeps a team notebook which includes agenda, minutes, parent and student conference forms, and other pertinent information.					
11. Our team has goals and objectives for the school year.					
12. Our team periodically evaluates its goals/objectives.					
13. Our team members use common planning time to correlate subject matter and to plan for interdisciplinary instruction.					

	Always	Frequently	Infrequently	Never	Comments
14. Our team members conduct face-to-face parent conferences during our team time.					
15. Our team members use team time to conduct student conferences.					
16. Our team discusses ways to use our academic block of time more effectively.					
17. Our team groups and regroups its students for instruction.					
18. Our team readily varies the schedule to accommodate teacher and student needs.					
19. Our team has an agenda for all team meetings.					
20. Our team follows the agend.					
21. Team planning time is kept strictly for team business.					
22. The team paces itself and allows for "ups" and "downs," cycles of hard work and relaxation.					
23. The team regularly takes time to provide outlets for members to share ideas and frustrations.					
24. Our team members inform the exploratory teachers about decisions reached at team meetings.					
25. Our team coordinates homework given to students so that it is spread out over the week.					
26. Our team coordinates test days so that students do not have more than one test on a given day.					
27. Our team has established common team procedures and policies for our students.					
28. Our team has established a team identity through the use of a team name, logo, team assemblies, etc.					
29. Two or more portions of our team plan and conduct several true interdisciplinary units.					
30. Our total team plans, implements, and evaluates at least two thematic units a year.					

Team Effectiveness Instrument

Part Two (Optional)

Team Meeting Observation Form

This form is to be used when a non-team member observes a team planning time. The results of this observation can be compared to the team's self-checklist. The numbers in parentheses refer to the number of related questions from the team's self-checklist. (part one)

Question	Yes	No	Comments
1. All team members present at the team meeting.(2)			
2. All team members arrived on time. (3)			
3. All team members stayed for the full meeting. (4)			
4. Team members discussed ways to best meet the needs of students. (5)			
5. The members of the team appear to support the efforts of the team leader. (7)			
6. Each member of the team played an active role during themeeting. (8)			
7. The team had a team notebook which included copies of agendas, minutes, parent and student conference forms, and other pertinent information. (10)			
8. Team members discussed correlating subjects and/or plans for interdisciplinary instruction. (13) (29)			
9. Each team member had an agenda. (19)			
10. Team members followed the agenda. (20)			
11. Ideas and frustrations were readily shared. (23)			
12. The team has a team name and there was evidence that team identity is strong. (28)			

Team Effectiveness Instrument

Part Three

Team Member Interview Form

This form is to be used when a non-team member is called in to interview selected team members regarding the effectiveness of the common planning time and the member's feelings regarding interdisciplinary team organization.

1. How do you feel in general about being a member of an interdisciplinary team?

2. What is the best thing about being a member of your team?

3. What is the most difficult thing about being a member of your team?

4. How do you feel about the effectiveness of your team meetings?

5. Tell me something about the face-to-face parent conferences conducted by your team.

6. Tell me something about the student conferences conducted by your team.

7. Tell me about how your team used the services of resource personnel such as counselors, house leaders, psychologists, and special education teachers.

8. Tell me about the coordination of instruction and scheduling on your team.

9. State three things that your team is doing to help meet the needs of your students.

10. State three things that your team does to meet the needs of the adult team members.

11. State three things that your team has done to build team identity with your students.

12. Any additional comments?

Instrument for Evaluation of Advisory Program Effectiveness

Part One

Teacher Self-Checklist

To be completed individually by each advisor.

Question	Yes	No	Comments
1. My school or district has developed a comprehensive advisory program complete with philosophy statement, goals, objectives, and activity suggestions.			
2. I have a copy of the full advisory plan or program for my grade level.			
3. The advisory program in my school has a name and a logo.			
4. Each student in my school has daily contact with his/her advisory teacher.			
5. Each student in my school begins his/her day with their advisory teacher.			
6. There is a person or group who coordinates, monitors, and evaluates the advisory program.			
7. The advisory activities are appropriate for students in my grade level.			
8. The weekly schedules of events for advisory is appropriate. (i.e. 1 day for silent reading, 1 day for special activities, 2 days for content, 1 day for study hall)			
9. I have more than enough advisory activities to choose from under any given topic.			
10. If I have an activity in my personal files that is appropriate for the advisory topic to be discussed, I am free to deviate from the activities in the advisory activities.			
11. The advisory activities require minimum use of paper and pencil and allow for free small or whole group discussion.			

Question	Yes	No	Comments
12. There are very few outside interruptions during advisory time. It is "sacred" and an important part of our day.			
13. The number of students in my advisory class is appropriate or satisfactory. (17-23).			
14. Every certificated person in my school is an advisory teacher with the exception of only a few persons. (i.e. perhaps not all administrators or all counselors)			
15. The majority of students enjoy advisory time.			
16. The majority of parents are supportive of the advisory program.			
17. The majority of faculty enjoy advisory time.			
18. I enjoy advisory time.			
19. I feel that the advisory program is beneficial to students.			
20. Affective education is an integral part of my school day.			

Instrument for Evaluation of Advisory Program Effectiveness

Part Two (Optional)

The Advisory Class Observation Form

This form is to be used when a person is called in to observe an advisory class. The results of this observation can be compared to the teachers self-checklist. The numbers in parentheses refer to the number of related questions from the team's self-checklist.

Question	Yes	No	Comments
1. The advisory teacher is in possession of a full copy of the advisory program for his/her grade level. (2)			
2. Advisory time occurs at the beginning of the day. (5)			
3. The advisory activity for this particular day seemed appropriate for these students. (7)			
4. The activity for the day was taken directly from a bank of suggested advisory activities in the manual.(9)			
5. The activity for the day was taken from the advisory teacher's personal files. (10)			
6. The activity required minimum use of paper and pencil and allowed for free small or whole group discussion.(11)			
7. There were very minimal or no outside interruptions during this advisory class. (12)			
8. The number of students in this advisory class is appropriate. (13)			
9. The students in this advisory class appeared to be enjoying themselves. (15)			
10. The teacher appeared to be enjoying his/herself. (18)			
11. The students appeared attentive and took part in the activity.			
12. The teacher appeared prepared for advisory class.			
13. The teacher participated in the activity with the students and shared his/her feelings.			
14. There seemed to be a caring atmosphere among students as well as from the teacher.			

Instrument for Evaluation of Advisory Program Effectiveness

Part Three

Teacher Interview Form

This form is to be used by an outside observer to interview selected advisory teachers regarding the effectiveness of the advisory program and the teacher's feelings toward the program.

1. How do you feel in general about the advisory program in your school?

2. What is the best thing about being an advisor?

3. What is the most difficult thing about being an advisor?

4. If you could change one thing regarding the advisory program at your school, what would you change?

5. What type of activities have been successful with your students.

6. What type of activities have been unsuccessful with your students.

7. Name three qualities that a successful advisor must possess.

8. State three "DO'S" for a successful advisor.

9. State three "DON'TS" for an advisor.

10. Do you feel that the advisory program at your school helps to meet the needs of your students? Please elaborate.

11. Any additional comments?

Instrument for Evaluation of Classroom Instruction

Part One

The Teacher Checklist

This checklist should be completed individually by the teacher prior to the observation period.

	Always	Frequently	Infrequently	Never	Comments
1. I have specific objectives written for each of my lessons.					
2. I regularly change my method of instruction or activity every 15 minutes or so for each lesson.					
3. I begin planned activities promptly and continue them until the end of the instruction period in each lesson.					
4. I let students know the purpose of each lesson.					
5. I relate the new ideas taught in class to earlier content taught.					
6. I give clear directions to students for each lesson.					
7. I plan to usemore than one modality in each lesson.					
8. I use varied resource materials in each lesson.					
9. I use varied instructional strategies in each lesson.					
10. I actively involvethe students in each lesson.					
11. I actively supervise students by circulating among them.					
12. I provide opportunities for students to develop effective oral communication skills in each lesson.					

	Always	Frequently	Infrequently	Never	Comments
13. I regularly ask questions on all levels of Bloom's Taxonomy.					
14. I provide time for students to practice a skill or apply the concept in each lesson.					
15. I have a procedure for determining if the objectives have been met in each lesson.					
16. I encourage feedback from my students in each lesson.					
17. I give specific and constructive feedback to students in each lesson.					
18. I keep students motivated to learn in each lesson.					
19. I use individual rewards or reinforcement for good behavior in each lesson.					
20. I am able to maintain an acceptable level of discipline.					
21. I always foster a positive learning environment.					

Instrument for Evaluation of Classroom Instruction

Part Two (Optional)

Teacher Observation Form

This form is to be used when an outside observer is called in to observe a teacher during an instructional period. The results of this observation can be compared to the teacher's self-checklist. The numbers in parentheses refer to the number of related questions from the teacher's self-checklist.

Question	Yes	No	Comments
1. Objectives were written down for the lesson. (1)			
2. Instructional period for lesson was 40-45 minutes. (2)			
3. Method of instruction was changed every 11-15 minutes within the lesson.			
4. Instruction began promptly and continued until end of designated period. (4)			
5. Students informed of purpose for lesson. (5)			
6. New ideas related to earlier content taught in lesson.(6)			
7. Clear directions given to student in lesson. (7)			
8. More than one modality addressed in lesson. (8)			
9. More than one resource used in delivery of lesson. (9)			
10. More than one instructional strategy used during lesson. (10)			
11. All students actively involved in lesson. (11)			
12. Teacher circulated among students during lesson. (12)			
13. Opportunities for oral communication skills provided throughout lesson. (13)			
14. Questions in at least four out of six levels of Bloom's Taxonomy used in lesson. (14)			
15. Practice in application of skills/concepts provided in lesson. (15)			

Question	Yes	No	Comments
16. Procedure for evaluating objectives evident in lesson. (16)			
17. Feedback from students encouraged in lesson. (17)			
18. Constructive feedback given to students during lesson. (18)			
19 Motivational techniques applied with students during lesson. (19)			
20. Individual reward and reinforcement used with students during lesson. (20)			
21. Acceptable level of discipline evident during lesson. (21)			
22. Positive learning environment fostered during lesson. (22)			

Instrument for Evaluation of Classroom Instruction

Part Three

Teacher Interview Form

This form is to be used by an outside observer with the teacher upon completion of both the teacher's self-checklist and the observation itself.

1. How do you determine your objectives for each lesson you teach?

2. How do you structure a typical 45 minute lesson?

3. Have you administered any modality, left brain/right brain, learning style, or interest inventories to your students this year? If so, how do you incorporate this information in your classroom?

4. How do you regularly select your teaching materials and resources for classroom instruction?

5. What percentage of classroom instruction depends on the textbook as a delivery system in any given week?

6. What percentage of classroom instruction incorporates each of the following instructional strategies during any given week:
   - _____ a.   Cooperative learning groups
   - _____ b.   Individualized instruction
   - _____ c.   Learning centers
   - _____ d.   Contracts
   - _____ e.   Independent study packages
   - _____ f.   Gaming and simulation
   - _____ g.   Lecture
   - _____ h.   Peer tutoring
   - _____ i.   Other (please specify)

7. How do you determine what level of questions to use with students during a given instructional session?

8. How do you know if your delivery system or teaching lesson has been successful?

9. What kind of student feedback do you regularly use in the classroom?

10. What techniques do you use most often to motivate students and how successful do you feel they are?

11. What techniques do you use most often to discipline students and how successful do you feel they are?

Open-Ended Interview Questions

1. Tell me about yourself.

2. What do you like best about your school?

3. If you could change one thing about your school, what would you change?

4. How do you feel about the quality of instruction that students are receiving at your school?

5. How do you feel about the exploratory program at your school?

6. How do you feel about the advisory program at your school?

7. How do you feel about the team organization at your school?

8. How do you feel about the extracurricular program offerings at your school such as sports, dances, clubs, intramurals, etc.?

9. How do you feel about the overall discipline at your school?

10. Please make any additional comments at this time.

Directions

(Generic — to use with the following surveys when utilizing computer answer sheets)

1. You must use a #2 pencil and completely fill in the circles on the green and white computer answer sheet.

2. Do not fill in the section labeled "Last Name," "FI," "MI," or "Social Security" on the green and white computer answer sheet.

3. In the first two columns of the "Section" area, fill in the number of years you have been at this school. (e.g. 01, or 11)

4. In the last two columns of the "Section" area, fill in your classification according to the following scale:

   01 = Student

   02 = Core Teacher (Social Studies, Science, Reading/Language Arts, Math)

   03 = Special Area Teacher (P.E., Art, Music, Media)

   04 = Counselor

   05 = Administrator

   06 = Parent/Guardian

   07 = Support Staff (Custodian, Secretary, etc.)

5. You are now ready to complete the survey. Please proceed but, be sure not to bend, fold, or staple the green and white computer answer form.

Thank you for your time and effort in this important endeavor.

Student Survey

Use the scale below to indicate how much you **agree** or disagree with the statements.

1 - strongly agree   2 - agree
3 - neither agree nor disagree   4 - disagree
5 - strongly disagree

Please leave an answer space blank if you do not know enough about the statement made.

1. I am happy with the academic opportunities my school is providing for me.

2. I am happy with the social opportunities my school is providing for me. (dances, clubs, etc.)

3. I am happy with the enrichment opportunities my school is providing for me. (music, art, athletics, etc.)

4. I like my school.

5. There are times during the school day when I can "run around," release some of my energy.

6. Students behave well in class.

7. Students behave well outside of class.

8. I feel safe at school.

9. I enjoy going to my school.

10. I feel that I belong at my school.

11. Adults at my school listen to each other.

12. The teachers work well together in my school.

13. Student behavior is appropriate.

14. The feeling at my middle school is positive.

15. I like working with a team of teachers.

16. I feel that my team of teachers helps me.

17. There is time during my school day when I can relax or study.

18. The number of classes I attend each day is just about right.

19. I like the master schedule in my school.

20. I feel that I have input about what happens to me at school.

21. I feel good about my non-academic classes.

22. I have an opportunity to learn the basic skills at my school. (math facts, reading, etc.)

23. I enjoy the time spent in my Advisor/Advisee class.

24. I like the Advisor/Advisee activities.

25. I feel that my Advisor/Advisee teacher cares about me.

26. I like the way my teachers teach me.

27. I like the subjects I am taking.

28. I feel that adults in my school listen to what I have to say.

29. Students at my school feel good about themselves.

30. Adults at my school feel good about themselves.

31. I like the new middle school programs such as Advisor/Advisee and the teams.

32. Fill in the #1 circle if you are female. Fill in the #2 circle if you are male.

33. Fill in your grade level according to the following scale:

    1 = grade 6   2 = grade 7   3 = grade 8

Faculty Survey

Use the scale below to indicate how much you agree or disagree with the statements.

1 - strongly agree   2 - agree
3 - neither agree nor disagree   4 - disagree
5 - strongly disagree

Please leave an answer space blank if you do not know enough about the statement made.

1. I am pleased with the academic opportunities this school is providing for students.

2. I am pleased with the social opportunities this school is providing for students. (dances, clubs etc.)

3. I am pleased with the enrichment opportunities this school is providing for students. (music, art, athletics, etc.)

4. This school is meeting the emotional needs of its students.

5. This school is meeting the physical needs of its students.

6. There is good discipline within classes.

7. There is good discipline on school grounds.

8. This school provides a safe environment for students.

9. I enjoy working at this school.

10. I feel that I am part of the school community.

11. Adults at this school listen to each other.

12. Teachers work well together in this school.

13. Student conduct is appropriate.

14. Our middle school atmosphere is positive.

15. The team organization in this school is helpful to teachers.

16. The team organization in this school is helpful to students.

17. As a teacher in this school, I have enough planning time.

18. I feel that the number of instructional periods assigned to me is appropriate.

19. The master schedule in this school is good and requires only minor changes.

20. I feel that I have input in the development of our master schedule.

21. The exploratory or elective program in our school is good.

22. This school provides opportunities for students to acquire basic academic skills.

23. I am pleased with the Advisor/Advisee schedule in this school.

24. I am pleased with the Advisor/Advisee activities in this school.

25. I feel that the Advisor/Advisee program in this school benefits our students.

26. I feel good about the quality of my classroom teaching.

27. I feel good about the subjects which I am teaching.

28. I feel that I have input regarding critical decisions made at my school.

29. Students at our school feel good about themselves.

30. Adults at our school feel good about themselves.

31. I support the middle school philosophy and programs.

32. If given the choice, I would choose to work in a school with a junior high philosophy, program, and schedule.

33. I enjoy working at this school more this year than in previous years.

34. I am pleased that my county has decided to implement middle school philosophy, programs, and schedules on a county wide basis.

35. Fill in the #1 circle if you are female. Fill in the #2 circle if you are male.

36. Fill in the grade level from which most of your students come according to the following scale:

          1 = grade 6   2 = grade 7

          3 = grade 8   4 = you deal with all grades

Counselor/Administrative Survey

Use the scale below to indicate how much you **agree** or **disagree** with the statements.

1 - strongly agree   2 - agree
3 - neither agree nor disagree   4 - disagree
5 - strongly disagree

Please leave an answer space blank if you do not know enough about the statement made.

1. I am pleased with the academic opportunities this school is providing for students.

2. I am pleased with the social opportunities this school is providing for students. (dances, clubs etc.)

3. I am pleased with the enrichment opportunities this school is providing for students. (music, art, athletics, etc.)

4. This school is meeting the emotional needs of its students.

5. This school is meeting the physical needs of its students.

6. There is good discipline within classes.

7. There is good discipline on school grounds.

8. This school provides a safe environment for students.

9. I enjoy working at this school.

10. I feel that I am part of the school community.

11. Adults at this school listen to each other.

12. Teachers work well together in this school.

13. Student conduct is appropriate.

14. Our middle school atmosphere is positive.

15. The team organization in this school is helpful to teachers.

16. The team organization in this school is helpful to students.

17. I feel that teachers in our school have enough planning time.

18. I feel that the duties assigned to me are fair and of a manageable nature.

19. The master schedule in this school is good and requires only minor changes.

20. I feel that I have input in the development of our master schedule.

21. The exploratory or elective program in our school is good.

22. This school provides opportunities for students to acquire basic academic skills.

23. I am pleased with the Advisor/Advisee schedule in this school.

24. I am pleased with the Advisor/Advisee activities in this school.

25. I feel that the Advisor/Advisee program in this school benefits our students.

26. I feel good about the quality of my work as a counselor or administrator.

27. I feel good about the courses offered to our students.

28. I feel that I have input regarding critical decisions made at my school.

29. Students at our school feel good about themselves.

30. Adults at our school feel good about themselves.

31. I support the middle school philosophy and programs.

32. If given the choice, I would choose to work in a school with a junior high philosophy, program, and schedule.

33. I enjoy working at this school more this year than in previous years.

34. I am pleased that my county has decided to implement middle school philosophy, programs, and schedules on a county wide basis.

Fill in the #1 circle if you are female. Fill in the #2 circle if you are male.

36. Fill in the grade level of students with which you work according to the following scale:

      1 = grade 6   2 = grade 7

      3 = grade 8   4 = you deal with all grades

Dear Parent/Guardian,

We, the staff, at _____ are in
the process of collecting information that will help us evaluate and improve our
school. We need your help to do this.

Please take a few moments to complete this survey, place it back in the enve-
lope, and return it to your child's advisor no later than _____

Also, please do not discuss this survey with your child while you are filling it
out. We want YOUR opinions at this time. Respond to all items with only (name
of child) in mind, even if you have other children in other schools. We are interested in your general impressions about the school rather than an evaluation of
specific teachers. If you would like to express more specific thoughts or concerns,
please include them in the comments section at the end of the survey.

Thank you in advance for your time and effort with this project. The
information gained will help strengthen the programs offered at your child's
school.

Sincerely,

Principal,

Parent Survey

Use the scale below to indicate how much you agree or disagree with the statements.

        1 - strongly agree   2 - agree
        3 - neither agree nor disagree   4 - disagree
        5 - strongly disagree

Please leave an answer space blank if you do not know enough about the statement made.

1. I am pleased with the academic opportunities this school is providing for my child.

2. I am pleased with the social opportunities this school is providing for my child . (parties, clubs etc.)

3. I am pleased with the enrichment opportunities this school is providing for my child. (music, art, athletics, etc.)

4. This school is meeting the emotional needs of my child.

5. This school is meeting the physical needs of my child.

6. There seems to be good discipline within classes.

7. There seems to be good discipline on school grounds.

8. This school provides a safe environment for my child.

9. I feel good about sending my child to this school.

10. I feel welcome at this school.

11. When a situation presents itself, I feel that people at this school listen to me.

12. Teachers work well together in this school.

13. Students conduct is appropriate.

14. Our middle school atmosphere is positive.

15. I like the new team organization at this school.

16. I feel that the new team organization in this school is good for students.

17. Teachers are well-prepared for their classes.

18. The number of classes my child takes is just fine.

19. The length of my child's school day is just fine.

20. I feel that I have input into what happens to my child at school.

21. The exploratory or elective program in this school is good.

22. This school provides opportunities for students to acquire basic academic skills.

23. I am pleased with the Advisor/Advisee schedule in this school.

24. I am pleased with the Advisor/Advisee activities in this school.

25. I feel that the Advisor/Advisee program in this school benefits our students.

26. I feel good about the quality of teaching at this school.

27. I feel good about the subjects my child is taking at this school.

28. I feel that I am allowed an opportunity for input regarding critical decisions made at my child's school.

29. Students and adults at our school feel good about themselves.

30. I support the middle school philosophy and programs.

31. Fill in the #1 circle if you are female. Fill in the #2 circle if you are male.

32. Fill in the grade level of your child according to the following scale:

1 = grade 6	2 = grade 7
3 = grade 8	4 = I have children in more than one grade level

Support Staff Survey

Use the scale below to indicate how much you agree or disagree with the statements.

1 - strongly agree   2 - agree
3 - neither agree nor disagree   4 - disagree
5 - strongly disagree

Please leave an answer space blank if you do not know enough about the statement made.

1. I am happy with the academic opportunities this school is providing for students.

2. I am happy with the social opportunities this school is providing for students. (dances, clubs etc.)

3. I am happy with the enrichment opportunities this school is providing for students. (music, art, athletics, etc.)

4. This school is meeting the emotional needs of its students.

5. This school is meeting the physical needs of its students.

6. There is good discipline within classes.

7. There is good discipline on school grounds.

8. This school provides a safe environment for students.

9. I enjoy working at this school.

10. I feel that I am part of the school community.

11. Adults at this school listen to each other.

12. Teachers work well together in this school.

13. Student conduct is appropriate.

14. Our middle school atmosphere is positive.

15. The team organization in this school is helpful to teachers.

16. The team organization in this school is helpful to students.

17. I feel that teachers in our school have enough planning time.

18. I feel that the duties assigned to me are fair and of a manageable nature.

19. The master schedule in this school is good and requires only minor changes.

20. I feel that I have input in the development of our master schedule.

21. The exploratory or elective program in our school is good.

22. This school provides opportunities for students to acquire basic academic skills.

23. I am pleased with the Advisor/Advise schedule in this school.

24. I am pleased with the Advisor/Advise activities in this school.

25. I feel that the Advisor/Advise program in this school benefits our students.

26. I feel good about the quality of my work.

27. I feel good about the courses offered to our students.

28. I feel that I have input regarding critical decisions made at my school.

29. Students at our school feel good about themselves.

30. Adults at our school feel good about themselves.

31. I support the middle school philosophy and programs.

32. If given the choice, I would choose to work in a school with a junior high philosophy, program, and schedule.

33. I enjoy working at this school more this year than in previous years.

34. I am pleased that my county has decided to implement middle school philosophy, programs, and schedules on a county wide basis.

35. Fill in the #1 circle if you are female. Fill in the #2 circle if you are male.

36. Fill in the grade level of students with which you work according to the following scale:

1 = grade 6	2 = grade 7
3 = grade 8	4 = you deal with all grades